Her

Jordyn Silkstone

BookLeaf
Publishing

Presentation by *BookLeaf Publishing*

Web: www.bookleafpub.com

E-mail: info@bookleafpub.com

ISBN: 978-93-95890-17-5

First edition 2022

*There is only one person I could dedicate
this to, and that is Her.*

ACKNOWLEDGEMENT

I would really like to thank my mom for always lending her ear to listen, especially when I have told her the same thoughts and feelings over and over again, for being my shoulder to cry on and the hand that always helped me back up. I would like to thank my best friend, Zoey. Without her I wouldn't have had the courage to finally walk away. To my new friends, Charlotte and Trinity for showing my friendship when I needed it most, and for helping to make Victoria a true home for me. I would like to thank my Dad, for being the one to help me apply to my dream school and reassuring me that my dreams are possible. I would also like to thank my old teachers, Mr. Homewood for being the first to spark my dream and love for writing, and Mr. Chan for continuing to nurture my dreams of writing and showing me that its possible to live them. Last, but not least, I'd like to thank my sister for always being my safe space and extra push. Without any of you, I would not be the person I am today.

PREFACE

This book is feels like a part of my journal for the past four years. Some of these pieces are rewritten poems, others are brand new and have never seen the light of day, but all of them are a little piece of my heart.

Five years ago, I met a girl and I fell in love. A year ago we finally put an end to our unhealthy relationship, and writing this book and getting all of those emotions onto paper helped my heal in a way I didn't think was possible.

Kissed

You've kissed the stars back into me,
pressed each one onto my tongue
and when I look at you
I feel like I've swallowed the sun.

The Poem I Gave with a Rose

She is a fire
not so easily extinguished.

She knows of darkness
as if it has been branded
onto the back of her hands.

Despite wicked rains,
she burns in red hot embers
denying the black it's
desolating void.

and when she ignites
she erupts like fireworks
leaving in your eyes, her trace
even after they've closed.

Sunbeam

I lay my head on her chest
her heartbeat is a sweet-sounding music
pulsing through my veins.
A vibration that lulls my turbulent thoughts to
peace.

She smiles with such a brilliance
Death hesitates, and wars could stop cold.
She places kisses on my skin
in the same way that clouds decorate the earth in
Fresh snow
it paints euphoria on my tongue.

She is the same grace that rises the sun in the
morning
and eases it to rest at dusk.
I find beauty imprinted onto her cheeks
written in pieces of the sun.

she made me wish I had saved the word Love

"I love you"
Has become an inadequate declaration to the
sensation of feelings that builds in my chest.

When I look into her eyes,
snd see the person beneath them,
Tidal Waves of affection and admiration
harbour behind my tongue.

To say love,
compares to:
I love the rain
I love strawberry ice cream
I love the smell of fresh brewed coffee in the
morning.

While worthwhile acknowledgements,
it is an injustice to how my heart stutters when
I see her sleepy blue eyes flutter in the morning,
how her bare skin feels against mine as she pulls
my body to hers.
Her breath tickles the top of my head
and my soul feels like it's found home.

Blue

I wish not to admit
There is darkness that holds my hand at night.
When it pulls me in
I am blinded by blackness,
Hanging into the void and tethered only by a
string.
And though it seems as if I will not get out,
Suddenly, I find blue.

Blue, like the way summer sun reflects off the
sea.
Blue like the strike of electricity through the
thunderous night sky,
Blue. Like my favorite pair of eyes.

It is her eyes
that pull me back from light lessness,
Her hands
that brush sweat slicked hair from my face.
Her lips
That touches mine, and draws breath back to my
lungs
It is her.
That anchors me back to reality.

Arguments

We go back and forth
Playing tricks
Harsh words like
little pin pricks
to draw blood from one another.
If we unintentionally
Start to break our peace
I still find love stitched into Sentiments
that are meant to be
A little bit more than shrapnel.
I think they really come from a place
Too soft,
A place that, too many times
The nails of others have dug into
Too hard.
A built-in self-defence mechanism
to push people away.
To not allow them to brand you
Like others once did.
We are after all
just broken people,
Remembering how to let a little light
Back in.

Beyond the walls

There is a sadness swimming within her pool
blue eyes.
I often wish I could take hold of it, pull it from
them
as if it was as easy as
pulling a loose thread
from her favorite sweater.

The walls she built around herself
are made of marble and granite.
Beyond them lies a monster
born from injustice and great sorrow.
It is armed with talons and teeth.

I approach the gate.
and it snarls.

"What's wrong?" I ask

Her sharp reply reverberates through me,
A lashing against some crime
I have never committed.
Old festering wounds.

The monster turns her anguish into fury,
and strikes out against my flesh because
I have come too close.

I have seen her.
I know her wrath
and I love her all the same.

Too Much

I wish that love was given, and taken
In equal measures
So that I could love her freely
And not left to wonder if she will love me back.

It is in isolation that my mind is most cruel.
My inner whispers grow louder,
Hurling my insecurities back at me.
Echoes reverberate off my skull.

I am not good enough to be loved by her.
I am not the one she truly wants.
I am temporary, a place holder.

This chaos begins, and I can think of nothing
else,
So please.
Forgive my constant requests for reassurance,
Forgive my anxious hands for seeking you out
when it is not wanted,
And understand that to me,
You are the stars in my night sky.
If you go,
I will be left in nothing but darkness.

The First Time She Left Me

To be chosen by her
was everything.

(and I'm holding my breath because
I'm not ready for it to be my first one without
you.)

To be left by her
was devastating.

Rose Colored Glasses

These days are long, but at night
I get to see you again in my dreams.
I see you the way I used to,
Before reality tapped me on the shoulder
And my eyes opened to the truth.

it's peaceful
remembering you that way.
There, I can still love you.
There, I can still be wrapped in your arms,
and there,
you still hold me
like I'm still yours.
I don't have to remember
Why
We are no longer together.

I wake up
and my dream of you,
will always be just that.

A dream

What it's like to drown

She is a breath of fresh air
and it's terrifying because
she had left, and I made my peace with death
within the darkness of these choppy waters
but here she is again,
Air
after drowning for so long.
I am afraid that this new life vest is faulty,
if I am submerged again
I will not come back up.
I won't want to.

Can you even call that love?

To be around her, was to love her.
Even after every pin prick
and gaping wounds that took weeks to heal
I couldn't help it.

I've spent days trying to get away,
luring my heart back into my chest.
While I was gone
everything I thought I'd healed
Ripped open
A huge hole
Punched through my chest.

How do you love someone
that constantly tears the flesh away from your
bones.
Do their band aids fix their inflicted bullet
wounds?
Does it make you forget about the blood?

Misguided Misconceptions

Being with her
Was living without gravity.
Finding out the sunset clouds,
Stained pink   and purple
Do taste like cotton candy.

She was a summer's breeze
Kissing across bare shoulders,
Blades of brilliant green grass
Threading through your hair.
That first bite of a crisp peach
On a hot balmy day.

In a blink,
An instant
Gravity is reality
One yank of a string and you are reeling,
Unravelling

It is not cotton candy clouds she's pressed to
your lips, it is
tongue pressed to the inside stuffing
Of a child's bear
Ripped open.
A blurred-out watercolour of childhood dreams.

She did not give you light, but instead
Snuffed out the candle burning within you,
A flame without fire

Tucked you into a blanket made of rustling
Withered leaves.
Mistook blood-soaked claws for a breeze.
And that unblemished skin of a peach,
you cut open,
And found it rotting from the inside.

She kissed you, and you swore you tasted sea
sprayed air
But can you taste it now?

The vile, wretched thing
Spat Down
The Back
Of Your Throat?

Recovery

I feel a storm brewing within my chest,
A low-pressure system built on everything I can
never say to her.
The blameful wind of her words, howls across
my skin
Shuddering against the glass bones of my rib
cage,
A cage that I had to put there
A fragile shelter for my beating heart.

She told me to follow my dreams,
Held my hand as together
we jumped
And just before my feet could plant themselves
back on solid ground
She let go.
Moving was the plan, but not in opposite
directions
The waves that rage and hurl salt off shorelines,
are different coastal oceans

She whispers broken lines and empty promises
into the wind,
As if the distance between her and I only began
to exist

When she put kilometres between us
she tells me I'm the one that moved
but she's the one that left home first.

I missed the days when my nose touched the soft
skin in the crook of her neck.
Arms wrapped around her ribs, and I could feel
her heartbeat beneath her flesh
But her cage has always been made of iron, and
steel.
How didn't I know I was giving my heart to
someone, who wouldn't give me theirs?

One day this whirlwind that creeps up my throat
Will be released from the flood gates of my teeth
I will taste lightning on my tongue

For when she send storming gusts
to whistle outside my window, and ask why I
went
I will remind her:
You told me to.

Birthday Candle Wishes

A part of me wishes that I could get
Just one more glimpse of her face,
While the rest of me entirely recoils at the mere thought
of running into her by accident.

I wish I could taste her lips once more,
Without feeling the echoes of the lies
Spun by her tongue, and the words that still,
Continue to pull me apart.

I simultaneously wish to be forever entwined to her fates
And yet wish to never have had our paths cross

I wish loving her,
And hating her
Didn't feel the exact same.

I wished I had walked away whole,
Like she did.
Because maybe that would mean
I didn't love her
Like she never loved me.

It's Easier for me to Hate you

It's easier for me to think of you as I saw you
last.
perfectly okay.
it keeps me from focusing on your absence
within these four walls of a home
I moved on to without you.
I will not focus on my empty hands
Without yours to hold.
The silence that rings so deafly,
Without your voice.

It is easier to picture you laughing,
Carefree and easy going,
Undisturbed by the disturbance of my presence,
or lack thereof.
Instead, I will think of how my absence never
really disturbed you at all.

I can count one, two, three times that you left me
And I never left you.
I will think of the looks you gave to beautiful
girls
And my jealousy.
you never truly saw me.
I will remember the holes

Punched into the drywall, and the metallic tang
of your bloody knuckles,
When your hands wrapped around my throat
I wondered
if you forgot about the seduction of it all.

You stripped me of my skin and left me bones.
Became my shelter when the only threat to me
was you.

It is easier to hate you
And what you did to me,
Then face the fact that,
Despite it all
You still feel like home.

Just One More Time

Just when you think
"I cannot survive again"
You put one foot in front of the other
You open your eyes
and you rise

A Whole Year Later

I no longer notice her lack of presence
In this home I've built for myself,
No longer waste time
Wondering where she is now.
I take comfort in the thought that
She doesn't know me anymore,
We are just strangers
Who've shared a past.

The One After Her

I can envision what it would be like to fall in
love with you.
The same way I used to dream of the ocean air,
and the golden sky before I finally found it.
I can see myself in your gentle arms
Feel the potential warmth of your affection
I think maybe you
Could be the first sunbeam of my morning skies,
after enduring
A darkness in which
I could not imagine an end.